A Baker's Dozen

13 Kitchen Quilts from American Jane

❀ BY SANDY KLOP ❀

A Baker's Dozen
13 Kitchen Quilts from American Jane
By Sandy Klop

Editor: Deb Rowden
Designer: Amy Robertson
Photography: Aaron T. Leimkuehler
Location Photography: Sandy Klop
Illustration: Eric Sears
Technical Editor: Christina DeArmond
Production assistance: Jo Ann Groves

Published by:
Kansas City Star Books
1729 Grand Blvd.
Kansas City, Missouri, USA 64108

First edition, first printing
ISBN: 978-1-935362-92-0

Library of Congress Control Number: 2011929108

Printed in the United States of America by Walsworth Publishing Co., Marceline, MO

To order copies, call StarInfo at (816) 234-4636 and say "Books."

About the Author

Sandy Klop is the owner and founder of American Jane Patterns. She also designs fabric for Moda. Sandy markets her patterns and kits on her website, www.americanjane.com. Her quilts have been featured on the covers of several quilting magazines and she lectures around the country on the subject, "The American Jane Story in Fabric." Her vintage fabric features an upbeat color palate, kid friendly themes and a French twist. Sandy's teaching is student-centered, drawing the best from each quilter.

Acknowledgements

I am very grateful to my mother—who taught me to sew—and my grandmother, for her sewing machine. My sister in law, Eileen, deserves a lot of credit for getting me connected to quilts. It is with deep gratitude I'd like to thank my son and husband for their constant support and partnership in this quilting business. I would also like to thank my mini group members, who have stood by me through many years to where I am today.

I am very grateful to the staff at The Kansas City Star for taking me on. A big thank you to Deb Rowden, my editor, for keeping me on track and pulling all the pieces together. Another big thank you to my book team—Amy, Aaron, Eric, Jo Ann and Christina for making me look good.

A special thanks to my friends Chickie Ricciardi, Donna and Doug Johnson for allowing and orchestrating photos at the cottage house in Carmel to convey the best look for my quilts. And thanks to Susan Peissner for the photography in her kitchen, ongoing support of my work, and for keeping me stylish.

Contents

12

JANUARY:
One Block,
One Cardinal

16

FEBRUARY:
Two Blocks,
Two Flower Baskets

20

MARCH:
Three Blocks,
Three French Hens

24

APRIL:
Four Blocks,
Four Flowers

28

MAY:
Five Blocks,
Five French Baskets

34

JUNE:
Six Blocks,
Six Summer Stars

38

JULY:
Seven Blocks,
Seven Sand Pails

42

AUGUST:
Eight Blocks,
Eight Medallion
Rounds

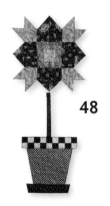

48

SEPTEMBER:
Nine Blocks,
Nine Flower Pots

52

OCTOBER:
Ten Blocks, Ten
Favorite Things

56

NOVEMBER:
Eleven Blocks,
Eleven Welcome
Pineapples

60

DECEMBER:
Twelve Blocks,
Twelve Peace
on Earth

64

Thirteen Blocks, A Baker's Dozen

Introduction

I started sewing when I was eight years old—on a little hand crank clamp-to-the-table Singer sewing machine making doll clothes. I graduated to my grandmother's Singer treadle machine when I was making my own clothes—even my wedding dress. Later I sewed for my children—clothes, dolls—and for my home.

But it wasn't until I was expecting my third child that I was introduced to quilts. No one in my family had made quilts. But my sister-in-law had taken a class in hand piecing, and thought I would be interested. I quickly shifted to machine piecing and then I was off and running.

It didn't take long for me to want to make every old quilt I saw. And then I did! And I haven't stopped yet…I'm almost to the point where I have too many quilts. In fact, I say this often, but I can't stop. I have quilts in every room of the house and even in the kitchen.

Why Quilts for the Kitchen?

The kitchen is where everyone shows up and hangs out: to cook, clean, play table games, do homework, read the paper, do projects, drink coffee or share a cup of tea.

There is usually not a lot of wall space, so if one were to put a quilt in the kitchen, it would probably be on the table. We have a small space between two doors where I hang a quilt and change it every month. You may find a spot over a window. Or, hang one from a plate holder by fanning one end - then push the other end through where the plate

would go and fan out the quilt. The weight of the quilt holds it in place.

Other ways to hang the quilts:
- On a shelf with a bar to the hold the quilt.
- By compression—between two pieces of wood held together by two knobs.
- Hanging with pins.
- Using a sleeve with a hidden holder.
- Using a curtain rod.

Sandy's Tips

CHOOSING FABRICS

The quilts in the book were made from fabric in my stash. I have an extensive stash—I suspect many of you do, too. It is much easier to choose many fabrics for a quilt than it is to select three that are just right. The more fabrics you have, the more they will work with each other. I have my fabric stored by color and by collections.

You will notice I love multi border patterned fabrics. I've used several in these quilts. It's a good way to make the fabric work for you. So, when I see a border fabric, I buy three yards if you can get four borders from it. If not, I buy six yards.

I also collect plaids, stripes, geometrics, stars and novelty fabrics. Of these fabrics I buy one half to one yard. I like running out of fabric so I have to substitute another. It's what draws me to the old quilts.

APPLIQUÉ

All the appliqué in this book is done with fusible web or interfacing. I machine stitch the fusible web pieces and hand appliqué the pieces done with interfacing.

General directions:

For appliqué, follow directions for whatever fusible web is available to you. However, general directions are as follows:

1. Trace all the pattern pieces for each fabric in a group.
2. Iron the fusible web onto the wrong side of the fabric.
3. Cut out each pattern on the traced line. Remove the paper backing.
4. Refer to available diagrams and arrange fabric on background and iron in place.
5. Stitch around each piece with an appliqué stitch using matching thread on top and a neutral in the bobbin.

For interfacing appliqué:

1. Trace the shape on the interfacing, then layer with fabric right side up.
2. Sew on the traced line. Trim ¼" around shape. Cut a small slit in the interfacing and trim.
3. Hand stitch in place.

MITERED BORDERS

Find the center of the border and center of the quilt and pin in place. Begin and end sewing ¼" from edges. Sew on all four borders. Next fold the quilt from a corner, wrong sides together, and align the raw edges of quilt with the borders pulled out straight and pattern matching.

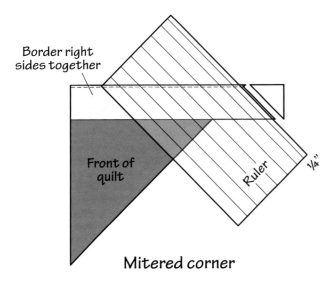

Border right sides together

Front of quilt

Ruler   ¼"

Mitered corner

Now lay the ruler's 45 degree line on the stitching line with the ¼" mark at the end of the stitching line. Cut the diagonal edge and stitch a ¼" seam. Press seam open. Repeat for remaining 3 corners.

If you have multiple borders, sew them together first then miter them all together, lining up each border so they'll all match.

QUILTING

Many of these quilts are small enough to quilt on a table top sewing machine. The center of the first quilt (Cardinal, page 12) was cross hatch stitched following the mini dots in the fabric. The others were quilted in an allover meandering stitch.

BINDING

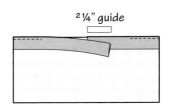

2¼" guide

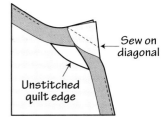

Sew on diagonal

Unstitched quilt edge

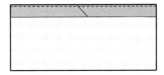

I love the part where you are almost finished.

* Cut binding strips, selvedge to selvedge, 2-¼" wide. The number of strips needed is given with each pattern.
* Join all the strips together with a diagonal seam, and press in one direction.
* Fold the strip in half lengthwise, wrong sides together.
* Align the raw edges together on a straight side of the quilt. Begin sewing 8" from the beginning of the strip and stop ¼" from the edge of the quilt.
* Remove the quilt from the machine and turn to the next side. Fold the binding strip straight up in line with the new side. If the corner is not a square corner (like on the Pineapple quilt, page 56) follow the direction or angle of the new side. Fold the strip down along the new edge with the fold at the last side edge. Begin sewing again ¼" from the edge, stopping ¼" again at the next corner.
* Continue around the quilt until you get within 12" of the beginning.
* Cut off ½" of the selvedge from the beginning of your binding strip.
* Take the end of the binding strip and layer it over the beginning. Use the selvedge piece to measure the overlap and cut the last strip, so the two strips overlap by the width of your strips.
* Pull the two ends to the side, place them right sides together, and sew on the diagonal. Trim to within ¼" of the seam. Then, finish sewing the binding to the quilt.
* Turn the folded edge over to the back and hand stitch to cover the seam line.

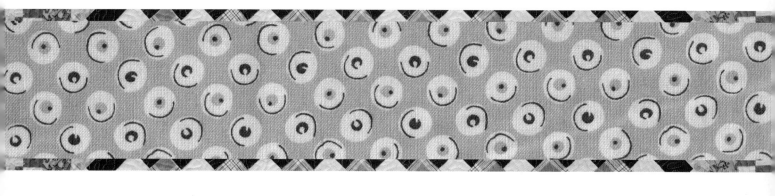

Projects

One Block, One Cardinal

Finished size: 18" x 27" • Templates for this quilt are on pages 70-71.

I love the idea of a clean slate—a new beginning, starting over, a clean piece of white paper. January does that for me. It's a new year, where we can begin again with the past behind and the future ahead. Here we are at the start again. Winters in Michigan made everything outside so black and white—the shape of skeletal trees against white snow, with the occasional cardinal. That was the inspiration for the January quilt.

FABRIC SUPPLIES

✳ Black pin dot	½ yard	
✳ White pin dot	⅝ yard	
✳ Black on white dot	¼ yard	
✳ White on black dot	¼ yard	
✳ Red pin dot	⅛ yard	
✳ 3 Greens	6" x 7"	
✳ 6 Reds	3 @ 2" x 4"	
	1 @ 4" x 8"	
	2 @ 2" x 5"	
✳ Brown	1" x 13"	
✳ Gold	2" x 2"	
✳ Black	2" x 3"	
✳ Eye-small polka dot	1" x 1"	
✳ Binding	included above	
✳ Backing	⅝ yard	
✳ Batting	23" x 31"	

CUTTING INSTRUCTIONS

From white pin dot fabric cut
- ✿ 1 piece, 15½" x 16-½"
- ✿ 2 strips, 1½" x width of fabric

From black on white dot fabric cut
- ✿ 36 squares, 1⅞" x 1⅞" and cut once on the diagonal
- ✿ 8 squares, 2½" x 2½"

From white on black dot fabric cut
- ✿ 12 squares, 1⅞" x 1⅞" and cut once on the diagonal
- ✿ 12 squares, 2⅞" x 2⅞" and cut once on the diagonal

From black pin dot fabric cut
- ✳ 3 strips, 1½" x width of fabric
- ✳ 3 strips, 2¼" x width of fabric for binding

From red pin dot fabric cut
- ✿ 1 strip, 1½" x width of fabric

MAKING THE CARDINAL BLOCK

Use the appliqué method of your choice. This quilt was made with fusible web.

For appliqué, follow directions for whatever fusible web is available to you.

General directions are as follows:
* Trace all pattern pieces for each fabric in a group.
* Iron the fusible web onto the wrong side of fabric.
* Cut out each pattern on the traced line. Remove the paper backing.
* Refer to quilt photo, arrange fabric on the background and iron in place.
* Stitch around each piece with an appliqué stitch using matching thread on top and a neutral in the bobbin.

Trace, fuse and appliqué all the pieces for the cardinal, branch, leaves and berries on the white pin dot background fabric. The background will finish 16" wide x 15" tall.

MAKING THE BLACK AND WHITE BLOCKS

* Sew 24 black on white triangles to the 24 small white on black triangles to make 24 half-square triangles.

* Sew the remaining black on white triangles to the 24 half-square triangles to make 24 large triangles with a light triangle sewn to each side of the dark portion of the half-square triangles.

* Sew the larger white on black triangles to these units to make 24 squares.

* Sew 8 of these squares together for the top border, changing directions in the middle.

BLOCK CENTERS

* Sew together the red pin dot strip and a black pin dot strip.

* Cut in half and sew together again.

* Subcut into 8 – 1½" segments.

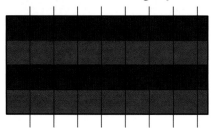

* Sew into 2 sets of 4 rows for each star center each alternating black and red.

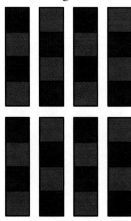

BLOCK ASSEMBLY

* Assemble the blocks as shown in the photo.

* Sew the blocks to the bottom of the cardinal block.

* Sew the top border to the cardinal block.

FINAL BORDER

* Sew the 2 black pin dot strips to the 2 white pin dot strips together in pairs. Subcut the paired strips into 44 – 1½" segments.

* Piece together the segments to make a row of 8 pairs for the top and bottom border and a row of 14 pairs minus one square for each side.

* Sew the top and bottom borders to the quilt, then the side borders.

FINISHING THE QUILT

* Quilt as desired and bind with the 2¼" wide strips.

Two Blocks, Two Flower Baskets

Finished size: 23" x 45" • Templates for this quilt are on pages 72-73.

February is such a fun short month, with a day off from school on the President's Birthday and Valentines Day. When I was growing up, Valentines Day was celebrated by making and trading valentines in the classroom. Nothing was done at home. One year my brother and two sisters received a present on Valentines Day wrapped in red tissue. Inside was red striped toothpaste and red mouthwash. Celebrate February with these two baskets of flowers, flags for the Presidents and some hearts.

FABRIC SUPPLIES

❄ Light background 1⅜ yards
❄ Red pin dot ⅓ yard
❄ 2 Blues ¼ yard
        6" x 9"
❄ Green stems fat quarter
❄ 7 Greens 2" x 5" each
❄ 6 Florals 4" x 6" each
❄ 6 Accents 2" x 3" each
❄ Blue star 3" x 6"
❄ Red/white stripe 5" x 8"
❄ Binding ½ yard red stripe
❄ Backing 1⅜ yards
❄ Batting 27" x 49"

CUTTING INSTRUCTIONS

From light background fabric cut
❀ 2 pieces, 16½" x 18½"
❀ 8 strips, 1½" x width of fabric
❀ 3 squares 1¾" x 1¾" and cut once on the diagonal.
❀ 23 squares, 2⅜" x 2⅜" and cut once on the diagonal
❀ 18 squares, 4⅛" x 4⅛" and cut twice on the diagonal

From red pin dot fabric cut
❀ 6 squares, 2½" x 2½"
❀ 4 strips, 1½" x width of fabric

From blue star fabric cut
❀ 2 pieces, 2¼" x 1¾"

From red/white stripe fabric cut
❀ 2 pieces, 1¾" x 2"
❀ 2 pieces, 1¾" x 3¾"

From wide red/white stripe fabric cut
❀ 4 strips, 2¼" x width of fabric for binding

MAKING THE FLOWER BLOCKS

Use the appliqué method of your choice. This quilt was made with fusible web.

For appliqué, follow directions for whatever fusible web is available to you.

General directions are as follows:
* Trace all pattern pieces for each fabric in a group.
* Iron the fusible web onto the wrong side of fabric.
* Cut out each pattern on the traced line. Remove paper backing.
* Refer to diagram and arrange fabric on quilt and iron in place.
* Stitch around each piece with an appliqué stitch using matching thread on top and a neutral in the bobbin.

* From the fat quarter stem fabric cut multiple ¼" strips on the diagonal. Sew the long edges right sides together. Cut a small slit 1" from an end on the folded side.

* Slide a bobby pin over the 1" above the slit, then down through the slit into the tube to turn right side out. Cut into short segments and stitch into place.

* To make the flags: sew the blue star fabric to the left of the smaller of the red/white stripe fabric pieces. Add the second stripe fabric below.

* Make the flag poles the same as the stems.

* For each block appliqué the flower pot, flowers, leaves and flag onto a large piece of background fabric.

MAKING THE FOUR PATCH BORDERS
* Take 4 red 1½" strips and 4 light background 1½" strips and sew them into pairs.
* Subcut into (83) 1½" segments to make 39 four patches and 3 single segments

* Make 3 sets of 5 four patches plus a single segment on point for the horizontal borders and 4 sets of 6 four patches on point for the vertical borders.

* Connect the four patches with setting triangles, the larger of the light background triangles.

* Use the middle size light background triangles for the corners of each four patch row except the right side of the 3 horizontal rows. For these corners use 2 of the smallest triangles.

* Use the middle size triangles for the sides of the large red corner posts.

* First sew the horizontal borders to the 2 appliquéd blocks.

* Next, sew 2 vertical borders together with 3 corner posts for each side.

* Then, sew the side borders to the quilt.

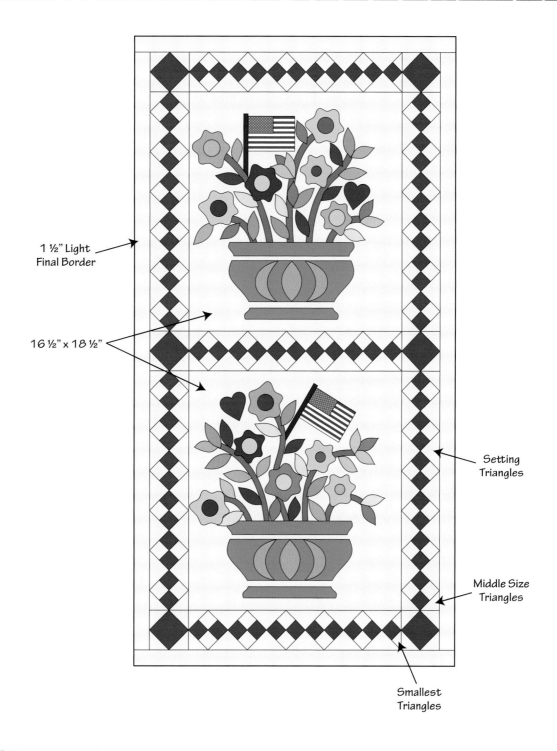

1 ½" Light
Final Border

16 ½" x 18 ½"

Setting
Triangles

Middle Size
Triangles

Smallest
Triangles

MAKING THE FINAL BORDER
From the 4 – 1½" light background strips make:
* 2 borders, 1½" x 44½" for the sides.
* 2 borders, 1½" x 22½" for the top and bottom.

* Sew the side borders to the quilt first, then the top and bottom borders.

FINISHING THE QUILT
* Quilt as desired and bind with the 2¼" wide strips.

MARCH:

Three Blocks, Three French Hens

Finished size: 28" x 55" • Templates for this quilt are on page 74.

The rooster may crow but it's the hen that delivers the goods. So how about scrambling some eggs for breakfast or bake something yummy to help take the chill off those March winds? The background fabrics are from my four-in-one Happy Campers line. If you can't find them in your local quilt shop, piece together something fun.

FABRIC SUPPLIES

3 backgrounds	3 fat quarters (4-1 fabrics)
3 hen fabrics	3@ 9" x 12"
Red crowns	3" x 6"
Gold beak & feet	4" x 6"
Eyes, dot pattern	1" x 3"
9 feather fabrics	9@ 4" x 6"
10 dark fabrics	fat eighth each 4 greens 2 yellow 2 reds 2 blues
Muslin	1½ yards
Cherry border	1½ yards, 3¼" wide for lengthwise print
Flower border	1¾ yards, 3½" wide for lengthwise print
Red pin dot	½ yard
Binding	Included in red pin dot
Backing	1¾ yards
Batting	32" x 59"

CUTTING INSTRUCTIONS

From the 3 background fabrics cut
- 3 squares, 12½" x 12½"

From assorted dark fabrics cut
- 20 squares, 2½" x 2½"
- 160 squares, 1½" x 1½" in 40 sets of 4

From muslin cut
- 160 rectangles, 1½" x 2½"
- 160 rectangles, 1½" x 4½"

From the cherry border cut
- 1 piece, 3¼" x 48½"

From the flower border cut
- 2 pieces, 3½" x 27¼"

From red pin dot fabric cut
- 2 strips, 1½" x width of fabric
- 5 strips, 2¼" x width of fabric for binding

MAKING THE HEN BLOCKS

Use the appliqué method of your choice. This quilt was made with fusible web.

For appliqué follow directions for whatever fusible web is available to you.

General directions are as follows:
* Trace all the pattern pieces for each fabric in a group.
* Iron the fusible web onto the wrong side of fabric.
* Cut out each pattern on the traced line. Remove paper backing.
* Refer to diagram and arrange fabric on quilt and iron in place.
* Stitch around each piece with an appliqué stitch using matching thread on the top and a neutral in the bobbin.

* Appliqué each hen onto a piece of background fabric.

MAKING THE SQUARE BLOCKS
* Sew a short muslin bar to each side of the (20) 2½" center squares.
* Sew a 1½" corner post to each end of the remaining short bars.
* Sew a new bar to the top and bottom of the center units matching the color of the bars.

* Sew a long muslin bar to each side of the new center units.
* Sew a 1-½" corner post to each end of the remaining long bars.

* Sew a new bar to the top and bottom of the center units matching the color of the bars.

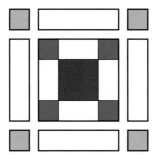

* Sew 2 completed blocks to the top and bottom of the hen blocks.
* Sew 8 blocks to each side of the hen blocks.

MAKING THE BORDERS
* Sew the cherry border to the left side of the quilt.

* Sew a flower border to the top and bottom of the quilt.

* From the 2 red pin dot strips make one border 1½" x 54½". Sew to the right side of the quilt.

FINISHING THE QUILT
* Quilt as desired and bind with the 2¼" wide strips.

APRIL:

Four Blocks,
Four Flowers

Finished size: 40" x 40" • Templates for this quilt are on page 75.

April is just four big flower blocks—all appliqué—translated to cut and paste. Bring some sunshine to the table and maybe a pot of flowers with a plate of cookies and a cup of tea.

FABRIC SUPPLIES

* Light background   1¾ yards
* Black stripe fabric   ½ yard
* Red fabric   ½ yard (includes binding)
* 2 Orange fabrics   4" x 4" & 4" x 12"
* 2 Yellow fabrics   4" x 8" & 8" x 12"
* 4 Blue fabrics   1½" x 4" each
* Black dot fabric   4" x 24"
* Light Green fabric   ⅜ yard
* Dark Green fabric   ⅜ yard
* Backing   1½ yards
* Batting   43" x 43"

CUTTING INSTRUCTIONS

From light background fabric cut
* 4 squares, 15½" x 15½"
* 4 squares, 5½" x 5½"
* 4 rectangles, 5½" x 30½"

From black stripe fabric cut on the diagonal
* 8 strips, 1¼" x width of fabric

From red fabric cut
* 4 strips, 2½" x width of fabric for binding

APPLIQUÉ OF THE FLOWERS AND LEAVES

* Using the 8 black stripe strips, sew right side together.
* Cut a small slit 1" from an end on the folded size. Slide a bobby pin over the 1" above the slit, then down through the slit into the tube to turn right side out.

Cut the strips into:
* (8) 13½" segments
* (8) 10" segments

* Fold the 4 large background squares corner to corner in both directions and press for placement.
* Use the appliqué method of your choice. This quilt was made with fusible web. For the appliqué, follow directions for whatever fusible web is available to you.

General directions are as follows:

* Trace all pattern pieces for each fabric in a group.
* Iron the fusible web onto the wrong side of fabric.
* Cut out each pattern on the traced line. Remove paper backing.
* Refer to diagram and arrange fabric on quilt and iron in place.
* Stitch around each piece with an appliqué stitch using matching the thread on top and a neutral in the bobbin.

* Trace, fuse, and appliqué the tulip flowers and leaves on the large background squares and border rectangles and corner squares.

* Sew the 4 large leaf blocks together and applique the round flowers, center leaves and the base of the tulips.

* Sew 2 rectangle borders to the sides of the quilt.
* Sew the corner squares to each side of the remaining 2 borders and sew to the top and bottom of the quilt.

FINISHING THE QUILT

* Quilt as desired and bind with the 2¼" wide strips.

15 ½" x 15 ½"   5 ½" x 30 ½"   5 ½" x 5 ½"

MAY:
Five Blocks, Five French Baskets

Finished size: 41" x 41" • Templates for this quilt are on page 76.

These baskets are brimming with color. If you didn't get a May basket for Mother's Day, here's a treat. I grant you permission to make your own Mother's Day baskets!

FABRIC SUPPLIES

* Light background   ½ yard
* Basket fabrics
      Bottoms   5 fat eighths
      Handles   2 fat eighths
      Triangles   (4) ⅛ yards
* Basket 1
      Light fabric   ⅛ yard
      Dark fabric   ⅛ yard
      Red   2" x 4" for berries
      Green   4" x 6" for leaves and stem
* Basket 2
      2 Dark fabrics   ⅛ yard each
* Basket 3
      5 Medium/Dark fabrics   ⅛ yard each
* Basket 4
      1 Light floral fabric   ⅛ yard
      2 Dark fabrics   ⅛ yard each
* Basket 5
      Light flower fabric   included below
* Sashing
* Red crossed fabric   ½ yard
* Setting Triangles
* Light flower fabric   ⅝ yard
* Border   ½ yard
* Binding (red pin dot)   ⅜ yard
* Backing   1½ yards
* Batting   45" x 45"

INTRODUCTION

There are 5 variations on these 12" baskets. All are constructed in a similar way.

The basket bottoms, handles and background pieces are same size for all the blocks. The band across the top of the basket is different for each one.

CUTTING INSTRUCTIONS

From basket background fabric cut
* A. (3) 9⅞" squares and cut once on the diagonal
* B. 10 rectangles, 2" x 9½"
* C. (3) 3⅞" squares and cut once on the diagonal

From each of 5 basket bottom fabrics cut
* D. (1) 6⅞" square and cut once on the diagonal
* E. (1) 2⅜" square and cut once on the diagonal

From each of 4 basket triangle fabrics cut
* F. (3) 3⅞" squares and cut once on the diagonal

For Basket #3 triangle fabrics cut
* G1. (2) 3⅜" squares and cut twice on the diagonal
* G2. (1) 3⅜" square and cut twice on the diagonal

From the 5 handle fabrics, cut out the handle template.

For Basket #1

From dark fabric cut:
- 1 strip, 1½" x width of fabric. Cut into thirds.
- Red for berries 2" x 4"
- Green for leaves, stem 4" x 6"

From light fabric cut:
- 1 strip, 1½" x width of fabric. Cut into thirds.

For Basket #2

From each of 2 dark fabrics cut:
- 1 strip, 2" x width of fabric

For Basket #3

From each of 3 medium fabrics cut:
- 1 strip, 2" x width of fabric

For Basket #4

From a light floral fabric cut:
- 1 strip, 1½" x width of fabric

From each of 2 dark fabrics cut:
- 1 strip, 1" x width of fabric

For Basket #5

From flower fabric cut:
- (3) 3½" squares

From the red sashing fabric cut:
- 8 pieces, 1" x 12½"
- 2 pieces, 1" x 13½"
- 2 pieces, 1" x 38½"

From setting triangle fabric cut:
- 1 square, 18¼" x 18¼" and cut twice on the diagonal.
- 2 squares, 9⅜" x 9⅜" and cut once on the diagonal for the 4 corners.

From border fabric cut:
4 strips, 3" x 38½"

From red pin dot fabric cut:
4 strips, 2¼" x width of fabric for binding

MAKING BASKET #1
- Sew a light strip in between 2 dark strips.
- Sew a dark strip in between 2 light strips.

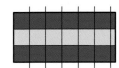

- Cut apart at 1½" intervals.
- Sew together to make 3 nine patches.

- Select 2 F triangles and put them right sides together.
- Measure 2" from the right angle and trim off excess.

- Sew the F triangles to the nine patches.
- Sew the D bottom to the nine patches.
- Sew an E footing to 2 background B's.
- Sew EB's to the basket.
- Add background C to the bottom.

- Appliqué the handle to background A.
- Sew to the top of the basket.
- Appliqué the cherries and leaves.

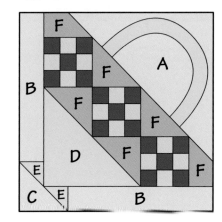

MAKING BASKET #2

* Sew 2 dark strips together.
* Cut 6 – 2" segments.

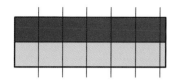

* Sew together to make 3 four patches.

* Select 2 F triangles and put them right sides together.
* Measure 2" from the right angle and trim off excess.

* Sew the F triangles to the four patches.
* Sew the D bottom to the four patches.
* Sew an E footing to 2 background B's.
* Sew EB's to the basket.
* Add background C to the bottom.

* Appliqué the handle to background A.
* Sew to the top of the basket.

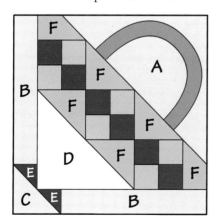

MAKING BASKET #3

* Sew 3 medium strips together.
* Cut 7 – 2" segments.

* Join the segments together diagonally adding G1 and G2 triangles to the ends.

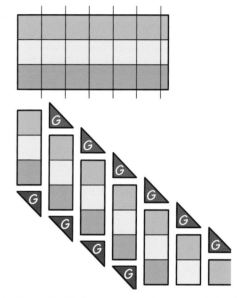

* Sew the D bottom to the top of the basket.
* Sew an E footing to 2 background B's.
* Sew EB's to the basket.
* Add background C to the bottom.

* Appliqué the handle to background A.
* Sew to the top of the basket.

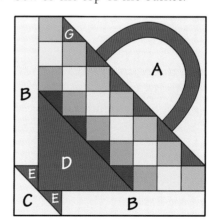

MAKING BASKET #4

From the light floral 1½"fabric strip cut:
❀ 3 segments, 1½" x 1½"

From one dark 1" strip cut:
❀ 6 segments, 1" x 1½"
❀ 6 segments, 1" x 2½"

✳ Sew a 1½" segment to each side of 3 light squares.
✳ Sew a 2½" segment to the top and bottom.

From the second dark 1" strip cut:
❀ 6 segments, 1" x 2½"
❀ 6 segments, 1" x 3½"

✳ Sew a 2½" segment to each side of the squares.
✳ Sew a 3½" segment to the top and bottom.

✳ Select 2 F triangles and put them right sides together.
✳ Measure 2" from the right angle and trim off excess.

✳ Sew the F triangles to the squares in a square.
✳ Sew the D bottom to the squares.
✳ Sew an E footing to 2 background B's.
✳ Sew EB's to the basket.
✳ Add background C to the bottom.

✳ Appliqué the handle to background A.
✳ Sew to the top of the basket.

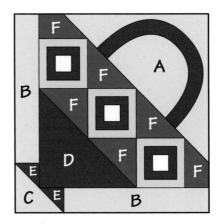

MAKING BASKET #5

✳ Select the 3 white flower 3½" squares.

✳ Select 2 F triangles and put them right sides together.
✳ Measure 2" from the right angle and trim off excess.

✳ Sew the F triangles to the 3 squares.
✳ Sew the D bottom to the squares.
✳ Sew an E footing to 2 background B's.
✳ Sew EB's to the basket.
✳ Add background C to the bottom.

✳ Appliqué the handle to background A.
✳ Sew to the top of the basket.

ADDING THE SASHING

* Sew a 12½" sashing strip to the lower left and upper right of Baskets, 1, 2, 4 and 5.
* Sew a 13½" sashing strip to the upper left of Basket 1 and to the lower right of Basket 5.

* Join Baskets 2, 3, and 4 together.
* Add the 2 – 38½" sashing strips.

ADDING THE SETTING TRIANGLES

* Sew a setting triangle to the lower left and upper right of Basket 1. Add a corner to the upper left.

* Add a corner to each end of Baskets 2, 3, and 4.

* Sew a setting triangle to the lower left and upper right of Basket 5. Add a corner to the lower right.

* Now sew the 3 basket units together on the diagonal.

ADDING THE BORDER

* Sew the 4 border strips in one continuous round. Begin sewing a border strip on one side, but do not finish the seam. Moving counter clockwise around the quilt, sew on remaining 3 borders. Then complete the first border.

FINISHING THE QUILT

* Quilt as desired and bind with the 2¼" wide strips.

ASSEMBLY DIAGRAM

Six Blocks, Six Summer Stars

Finished size: 30" x 40" • Finished block: 7½" • Note: There are no templates for this quilt.

Summer is here so let's celebrate with stars. Each star is different so dig into your stash and find those soft, tangy summer day colors. There are florals with plaids, checks and stripes. I love those combinations.

FABRIC SUPPLIES

* ❋ Scraps: As small as 3" and as large as 6½" Florals, geometrics, checks, plaids, dots, stripes
* ❋ Assorted 2½" strips
* ❋ Light inner border   ⅛ yard
* ❋ Binding (grid)   ⅓ yard
* ❋ Backing   1 yard
* ❋ Batting   34" x 44"

CUTTING INSTRUCTIONS

For each star
From light fabric cut:
* ✿ 4 squares, 3" x 3" for corners

From floral fabric cut:
* ✿ 1 square, 3" x 3" for centers

From fabric A cut:
* ✿ 1 square, 3¾" x 3¾" and cut twice on the diagonal

From fabric B cut:
* ✿ 1 square, 3¾" x 3¾" and cut twice on the diagonal

From fabric C cut:
* ✿ 2 squares, 3¾" x 3¾" and cut twice on the diagonal

For the framing of all the stars
From assorted fabrics cut:
* ✿ 12 squares, 6½" x 6½" and cut once on the diagonal

From inner border fabric cut
* ✿ 2 pieces, 1" x 32" for the sides
* ✿ 2 pieces, 1" x 22½" for the top and bottom

From half-square triangle border fabric cut
- 58 squares, 2⅞" x 2⅞" and cut once on the diagonal

From final border 2-½" strip fabric cut
- 3 strips, size varies, to equal 26½" for the top border
- 4 strips, size varies, to equal 38½" for the right side border
- 2 strips, size varies, to equal 28½" for the bottom border
- 4 strips, size varies, to equal 40½" for the left side border

From binding fabric cut
- 4 strips, 2¼" x width of fabric

MAKING EACH STAR
* Sew A and B triangles to C triangles with the C triangle on the bottom.

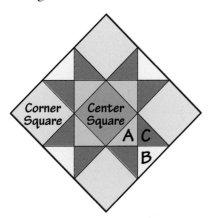

* Sew A/C unit to B/C units 4 times.

* Sew an ABC unit to each side of a center square.

* Sew a corner square to each side of an ABC unit and add to the top and bottom of the center square.

FRAMING EACH STAR
* Sew a framing triangle to each side of a star block.

ASSEMBLING THE BLOCKS
* Square up the 6 blocks to 11".

* Sew into 2 columns of 3 blocks.

ADDING THE INNER BORDER
* Sew the 2 longer inner border pieces to the sides of the quilt.
* Sew the 2 shorter inner border pieces to the top and bottom.

ADDING THE HALF-SQUARE TRIANGLE BORDER
* Sew 116 triangles into pairs to make 58 half-square triangles.

* Sew 2 rows of 11 half-square triangles for the top and bottom borders.

* Sew 2 rows of 18 half-square triangles for the sides changing directions of the first half-square triangle in one row and the last half-square triangle in the other row. For each row, sew slightly smaller seams for 8 of the half-square triangles to add ½" to the length of the row.

ADDING THE FINAL BORDER
* First sew the top border to the quilt.
* Then add the right side border.
* Sew the bottom border to the quilt.
* Add the left side border to finish the quilt.

FINISHING THE QUILT
* Quilt as desired and bind with the 2¼" wide strips.

Seven Blocks, Seven Sand Pails

Finished size: 36" x 48" • Templates for this quilt are on pages 77-78.

On the beach or at the kitchen table, listen for the ocean's roar and feel the breeze kiss your cheek. I always think of Robert Louis Stevenson's poem:

When I was down beside the sea
A wooden spade they gave to me
To dig the sandy shore
My holes were empty as a cup
In every hole the sea came up
Till it would come no more.

FABRIC SUPPLIES

* Blue background — ¾ yard
* Sand background — ¾ yard
* Beige — ⅜ yard
* Taupe — ¼ yard
* Novelty prints — 7 fat eighths
* Coordinating fabrics and pinwheels — 21 fat eighths
* Blue binding — ⅜ yard
* Backing — 1½ yards
* Batting — 40" x 52"

CUTTING INSTRUCTIONS

From blue background fabric cut
* 7 rectangles, 8½" x 12½"

From sand background fabric cut
* A. 1 rectangle, 4½" x 12½"
* B. 3 rectangles, 5½" x 12½"
* C. 3 rectangles, 3½" x 12½"
* D. 1 rectangle, 6½" x 12½"
* 3 strips, 2" x width of fabric

From beige fabric cut
* 5 strips, 2" x width of fabric

From taupe fabric cut
* 2 strips, 2" x width of fabric

From assorted fabrics cut
* 80 squares, 2⅜" x 2⅜" and cut once on the diagonal

Seven Blocks, Seven Sand Pails continued

From blue binding fabric cut
* 5 strips, 2¼" x width of fabric

APPLIQUÉ OF THE PAILS
* Trace, fuse and appliqué the pails on the blue backgrounds and prepare the shovels for appliqué later.

MAKING THE CHECKERBOARDS
* Sew the beige strips to each sand and taupe strips to make 5 pairs.
* Subcut into 2" segments.
* Sew the segments into 2 sets of 20 segments.
* Sew remaining segments together to make 32 four patches.
* Sew into 4 sets of 3 four patches and 4 sets of 2 four patches.
* 12 single four patches will remain.

MAKING THE PINWHEELS
* Using the assorted 160 triangles for each pinwheel, sew 4 of one fabric to 4 of another fabric to make 4 half-square triangles.
* Sew these together to make 20 pinwheels.

ASSEMBLY OF THE QUILT
* Sew 3 sand rectangles on the sides of 2 pail blocks for the first row—one A size, and 2 B sizes.
* Sew 2 sand rectangles in between three pail blocks for the second row—2 C sizes.
* Sew 3 sand rectangles on the sides of 2 pail blocks for the third row—B size, C size and D size.
* Sew 1 checkerboard set to the bottom of the first row of pails.
* Appliqué 3 shovels onto the first row.
* Sew the second checkerboard set to the bottom of the second row of pails.
* Sew the second row of pails to the bottom of the first row of pails.
* Appliqué 2 shovels onto the second row.
* Appliqué 2 shovels onto the third row.
* Sew the third row of pails to the bottom of the second row.

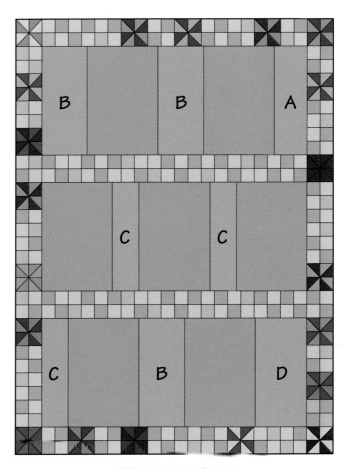

ASSEMBLY DIAGRAM

ADDING THE PINWHEEL BORDER

* Construct each side border with 5 pinwheels and a set of 3 four patches, a set of 2 four patches and 4 single four patches.

* Sew the side borders to the quilt.

* Construct each top and bottom border with 5 pinwheels and a set of 3 four patches, a set of 2 four patches, and 2 single four patches.

* Sew the top and bottom borders to the quilt.

FINISHING THE QUILT

* Quilt as desired and bind with the 2¼" wide strips.

Eight Blocks, Eight Medallion Rounds

Finished size: 47½" x 47½" • Template for this quilt is on page 44.

We have many August birthdays in our family, so I feel like I am going round and round. Over the eight rounds, some are easy and some are a little more work, but there is something new at every turn—just the way life is. I used a few of my border stripe fabrics here.

FABRIC SUPPLIES

❋ Basket fabrics	(4) 12" squares
❋ Red background	½ yard
❋ Light background	½ yard
❋ Second round fabric	⅝ yard
❋ Light print	¼ yard
❋ Medium pinks	To total ¼ yard
❋ Dark Yellow print	¼ yard
❋ Green plaid	¼ yard
❋ Yellow print	¼ yard
❋ Green leaf print	¼ yard
❋ Blue fabric	¾ yard
❋ White pin dot	¾ yard
❋ Red print	¾ yard
❋ Green binding	½ yard
❋ Backing	3 yards
❋ Batting	52" x 52"

CUTTING INSTRUCTIONS

From both light and red background fabric cut
- A. 1 square, 6⅛" x 6⅛" and cut once on the diagonal
- C. 4 rectangles, 2¼" x 4"
- E. 1 square, 4⅜" x 4⅜" and cut once on the diagonal

From each of 4 basket fabrics cut
- B. 1 square, 6⅛" x 6⅛" and cut once on the diagonal
- D. 1 square, 2⅝" x 2⅝" and cut once on the diagonal
- F. 1 square, 3½" 3½" for the basket handle

From second round fabric cut
- 4 strips, 4¾" x 24"

From light print fabric cut
- 38 squares, 2⅝" x 2⅝" and cut once on the diagonal

From medium pink fabrics cut
- 38 squares, 2⅝" x 2⅝" and cut once on the diagonal

From dark yellow print fabric cut
- 2 strips, 1¾" x 25½" for the sides
- 2 strips, 1¾" x 28" for the top and bottom

From light fabric cut
- 4 strips, 1¾" x width of fabric

From red fabric cut
- 4 strips, 1¾" x width of fabric

From green plaid fabric cut
- 8 squares, 4¾" x 4¾" and cut twice on the diagonal

From yellow print fabric cut
- 8 squares, 4¾" x 4¾" and cut twice on the diagonal
- 2 squares, 4⅜" x 4⅜" and cut once on the diagonal for corners

From green leaf print fabric cut
- 2 strips, 1¾" x 35" this is so the pieced border will fit correctly
- 2 strips, 1¾" x 37½" this is so next pieced border will fit correctly

From blue fabric cut
- 15 strips, 1½" x width of fabric

From white pin dot fabric cut
- 12 strips, 1½" x width of fabric

From red print fabric cut
- 5 strips, 2¼" x width of fabric to make
- 2 borders, 2¼" x 43½" for the sides
- 2 borders, 2¼" x 47" for the top and bottom

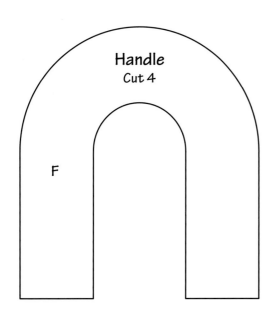

Handle
Cut 4

F

From green binding fabric cut
- 5 strips, 2¼" x width of fabric

ROUND ONE: THE FOUR BASKETS

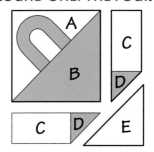

* To make the basket handles make a freezer paper template of handle F with 3 layers.
* Iron onto the 3½" square handle fabric.
* Trim fabric ¼" beyond the template.
* Clip the inside curve several times. Paint ¼" edge with spray starch and press around the handle template.
* Use a seam ripper to assist bringing the edge around. Let cool.

* Appliqué the handles to the large red and white triangle A's.

* Sew the D triangles to the C rectangles.
* Sew these to the B triangles.
* Add the E triangles to the bottom and A handles to the top.

* Sew the 4 baskets together to make the center square.

ROUND TWO: MULTIPLE BORDER FABRIC
* Sew the 4 strips to the center square.
* Miter the corners to the quilt.

ROUND THREE: HALF-SQUARE TRIANGLES
* Sew the light print triangles to the medium pink triangles to make 76 half-square triangles. Square up to 1¾".

* Sew 18 half-square triangles to the sides of the quilt and sew 20 half-square triangles to the top and bottom.

ROUND FOUR: DARK YELLOW PRINT

* Sew the shorter print borders to the sides of the quilt and the longer ones to the top and bottom.

ROUND FIVE: 36 FOUR PATCHES

* Sew the 4 red strips and the 4 light strips into pairs.
* Subcut into (72) 1¾" segments.
* Sew into 36 four patches.

* Construct 4 rows of 9 four patches, with 8 green plaid inside triangles and 8 yellow print outside triangles.

* Sew the rows to the 4 sides of the quilt, stopping ¼" from the corners, then sew the mitered corners. Add the corner triangles to the quilt.

ROUND SIX: GREEN LEAF PRINT

* Sew the shorter print borders to the sides of the quilt and the longer ones to the top and bottom.

ROUND SEVEN: CHECKERBOARD

Sew the (15) 1½" blue strips to the (12) 1½" light strips in the following manner:

* Sew 6 triads, dark, light, dark and 3 triads, light, dark, light.

* Subcut into 1½" segments.

* Sew into 2 sets of 37 units.

* Sew one set of 37 units to each side of the quilt. Sew a set of 43 units to the top and bottom.

ROUND EIGHT: RED PRINT

* Sew the shorter red print strips to the sides of the quilt.
* Sew the longer ones to the top and bottom.

FINISHING THE QUILT

* Quilt as desired and bind with the 2¼" wide strips.

ASSEMBLY DIAGRAM

Nine Blocks, Nine Flower Pots

Finished size: 39" x 46½" • Templates for this quilt are on page 79.

The days are warm but summer is fading, so time to bring the pots inside.
You'll have flowers all year long when you set these pots in your window sill.

FABRIC SUPPLIES

❋ Light background	⅞ yard
❋ Flower centers	6" square
❋ Greens	(9) 9" squares
❋ Prints	(9) 9" squares
❋ Accents	(9) 4" squares
❋ Geometrics	(9) 5" squares
❋ Trims	(9) 1½" x 6"
❋ Bases	(9) 1½" x 5"
❋ Brown stems	5" x 5"
❋ Light Brown sashing	¼ yard
❋ Dark Brown sashing	¼ yard
❋ Blue floral	½ yard
❋ Dark Blue	¾ yard
❋	(includes binding)
❋ Backing	1½ yards
❋ Batting	43" x 51"

CUTTING INSTRUCTIONS

From light background fabric cut
❀ A. 36 squares, 1½" x 1½" for all 9 flowers
❀ C. 72 squares, 1⅞" x 1⅞" and cut once on the diagonal
❀ H. 9 rectangles, 6½" x 8½"

From 9 different green fabrics cut
❀ B. 4 squares, 1⅞" x 1⅞" and cut once on the diagonal
❀ D. 4 squares, 1½" x 1½"

From 9 different print fabrics cut
❀ e. 4 squares, 1⅞" x 1⅞" and cut once on the diagonal
❀ E. 4 rectangles, 1½" x 2½"

From 9 different accent fabrics cut
❀ f. 2 rectangles, 1" x 1½"
❀ F. 2 rectangles, 1" x 2½"

From 9 flower center fabrics cut
❀ G. 9 squares, 1½" x 1½"

From light brown sashing fabric cut
❀ 9 rectangles, 1½" x 16½"
❀ 1 rectangle, 1½" x 23"

From dark brown sashing fabric cut
❀ 9 rectangles, 1½" x 8½"
❀ 1 rectangle, 2" x 45½"

From blue floral fabric cut

❀ 2 pieces, 6¼" x 42½"

From dark blue fabric cut

❀ 4 pieces, 1¾" x 42½"

❀ 4 pieces, 2½" x 8¾"

❀ 5 strips, 2¼" x width of fabric for binding

ASSEMBLY OF THE FLOWERS

✳ Sew f and F rectangles to the center G's.

✳ Sew 2 E rectangles to the center sides.

✳ Sew D squares to the ends of 2 E rectangles.

✳ Sew D/E to the top and bottom of the center.

✳ Make half-square triangles of C and e triangles and B and C triangles.

✳ Sew C/e half-square triangles together.

✳ Sew B/C half-square triangles to the ends of these rectangles.

✳ Sew 2 B/C/C/e rectangles to the sides of the center.

✳ Sew 2 A squares to the ends of 2 B/C/C/e rectangles.

✳ Add these to the top and bottom of the center.

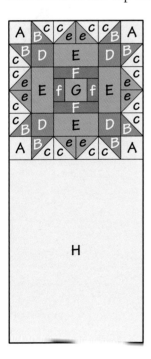

APPLIQUÉ OF THE FLOWER POTS

✳ Appliqué a pot, trim and stem to the bottom of the background rectangles.

✳ Reserve the bases until the blocks are pieced to the sashing.

✳ Sew a light background rectangle to the bottom of each flower.

ADDING THE SASHING

✳ Sew a light brown sashing rectangle to the right side of each flower block.

✳ Sew a dark brown sashing rectangle to the bottom of each block.

✳ Miter the right corners where the two sashing pieces come together.

✳ Appliqué the bases to the bottom of the pots.

ASSEMBLY OF THE FLOWER POTS

✳ Sew the completed flower blocks together in 3 rows of 3 blocks.

✳ Sew the long dark brown sashing strip to the left side of the quilt.

✳ Add the remaining light brown sashing piece to the top of the quilt.

MAKING THE SIDE BORDERS

✳ Sew a long dark blue piece to each side of the blue floral fabric.

✳ Sew a short dark blue piece to the top and bottom of these units.

✳ Sew each completed border to the sides of the quilt.

FINISHING THE QUILT

✳ Quilt as desired and bind with the 2¼" wide strips.

Ten Blocks, Ten Favorite Things

Finished size: 27½" x 47½" • Templates for this quilt are on pages 80-84.

Here are some of my favorite things for a French kitchen. Sunflowers, of course, chickens, tea, olive oil, fruit, fleur de lys and the green tea kettle. The checked shelf trim matches the border of my dishes. You have more of those border stripes. So much better than an overall pattern.

FABRIC SUPPLIES

* Background Fabric
#1 Taupe	⅝ yard
#2 Light	5" x 7"
#3 Blue	6" x 7"
#4 Light	7" x 7"
#5 Light	9" x 12"
#6 Blue	8" x 9"
#7 Light	7" x 7"

* Multicolored Borders
#1 Light Blue floral	6" x 25"
#2 Yellow floral	4" x 15"
#3 White/Red floral*	2½ yards
Red fabric	¼ yard
Muslin	¼ yard

* Assorted scraps from 3" to 10" square
French hens	5 fabrics each
Sunflower	4 fabrics
Stem	1" x 19"
Lime	3 fabrics
Pear	3 fabrics
Cherries	3 fabrics
Teapot	3 fabrics
Olive Oil Jar	4 fabrics
Beehive	2 fabrics
Fleur de lys	1 fabric

* Red binding ⅜ yard
* Backing 1½ yards
* Batting 31" x 52"

*For lengthwise cutting, otherwise ⅓ yard is needed

CUTTING INSTRUCTIONS

From background fabric #1 cut
* A. 8½" x 23½"
* B. 9½" x 23¾"
* C. 4½" x 8½"

From background fabric #2 cut
* 1 piece, 4½" x 6½"

From background fabric #3 cut
* 1 piece, 5½" x 6½"

From background fabric #4 cut
* 1 piece, 5½" x 6½"

From background fabric #5 cut
* 1 piece, 10½ x 8½"

From background fabric #6 cut
* 1 piece, 8½" x 6¾"

From background fabric #7 cut
* 1 piece, 6½" x 6¾"

From red fabric cut
1 strip, ¾" x width of fabric
3 strips, 1½" x width of fabric

From muslin cut
- 1 strip, ⅞" x width of fabric
- 4 strips, 1½" x width of fabric

From multicolored border #1 cut
- 1 piece, 4¾" x 23½"

From multicolored border #2 cut
- 1 piece, 3½" x 14½"

From multicolored border #3 cut
- 1 piece, 4½"x 29"
- 1 piece, 4½" x 49"

From red binding fabric cut
- 4 strips, 2¼" x width of fabric

APPLIQUÉ ALL OF THE ITEMS
- Appliqué the 3 French hens to background #1A.
- Appliqué the sunflower to background #1B.
- Appliqué the olive oil jar to background #1C.
- Appliqué the lime to background #2.
- Appliqué the pear to background #3.
- Appliqué the cherries to background #4.
- Appliqué the tea kettle to background #5
- Appliqué the bee hive/bee to background #6.
- Appliqué the Fleur de lys to background #7.

- Sew the lime, pear, and cherries together.
- Sew the tea kettle and olive oil jar together.
- Add to the bottom of the fruit row.

CHECKED SASHING
From (2) 1½" muslin strips subcut into:
- 4 squares, 1½" x 1½".
- 4 rectangles, 1½" 2½".
- 6 rectangles, 1½" x 3½".
- 6 rectangles, 1½" x 5½".

- Cut the ⅞" muslin strip in half.
- Cut the ¾" red strip in half.

- Sew a muslin strip to each side of a red strip.
- Subcut into 8 squares, 1½" x 1½".

- From (1) 1½" red strip subcut into:
- 24 squares, 1½" x 1½".

- From remaining muslin and red strips sew into pairs and subcut into 1½" segments.

- Sew into 2 sets of 2 rows of checks of 23 segments each.

- To make the third row of checkered sashing, sew a red square to each side of the 8 red/white squares.

- Connect 4 of these units with (3) 1½" x 3½" pieces and add a muslin square to each end of the row.

- Repeat for the other third row.

- For the fourth row sew a 1½" x 2½" muslin piece on each end with 4 red squares separated by 1½" x 5½" muslin pieces.

ADDING THE MULTICOLORED BORDERS AND QUILT ASSEMBLY
- Sew multicolored border #1 to the bottom of one checkerboard sashing and sew this unit to the bottom of the 3 French hens.

- Sew multicolored border #2 to the bottom of the fruit and tea kettle/olive oil jar unit.

- Add the bee hive and fleur de lys to the bottom of this unit.

* Sew the sunflower to the left this last unit.

* Sew the second checkerboard sashing to the bottom of this unit.

* Sew this last unit to the bottom of the upper portion of the quilt.

* Miter the 2 multicolored borders #3 to the left and bottom of the quilt.

FINISHING THE QUILT
* Quilt as desired and bind with the 2¼" wide strips.

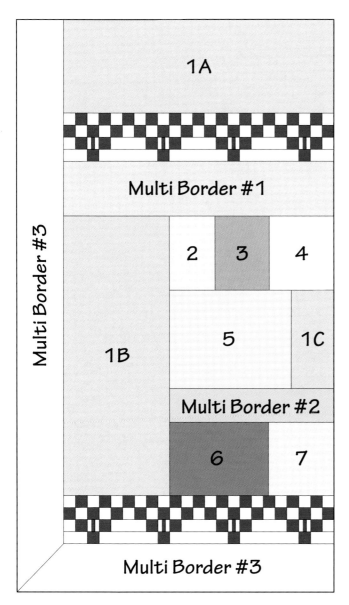

ASSEMBLY DIAGRAM

NOVEMBER:
Eleven Blocks, Eleven Welcome Pineapples

Finished size: 27" x 62" • Templates for this quilt are on page 85.

Brrr, it's cold outside—time to trim the house to welcome family and friends for festive dinners and cozy time by the fireplace. The pineapple has long been the symbol of welcome. Center these pineapples on the table, the buffet, or a mantle.

FABRIC SUPPLIES

* ❋ Light background A   ½ yard
* ❋ Medium background B   ½ yard
* ❋ 11 assorted Yellows   6" x 7" each
* ❋ Dark Green   ⅛ yard
* ❋ Light Green   ⅛ yard
* ❋ Border print stripe   2¼ yards
* ❋ Red binding   ⅜ yard
* ❋ Backing   1⅞ yards
* ❋ Batting   31" x 64"

CUTTING INSTRUCTIONS

From background A fabric cut
* ✿ 8 squares, 8½" x 8½"

From background B fabric cut
* ✿ 5 squares, 8½" x 8½"

From the border fabric cut
* ✿ 2 pieces, 2¾" x length of fabric
* ✿ 6 triangles from the red section

* ✳ Mark a 12½" square ruler with tape from 9" to 9" diagonally.
* ✳ Use corner for a template to cut out the triangles.

From red binding fabric cut
* ✿ 5 strips, 2¼" x width of fabric.

APPLIQUÉ 11 PINEAPPLES

✳ Trace, fuse and appliqué 8 pineapples to background A and 3 pineapples to background B.

ASSEMBLY OF THE QUILT

✳ Sew the pineapple blocks together in diagonal rows with the setting triangles.

SEWING THE BORDERS TO THE QUILT

✳ Cut 39" off each border strip. Sew each piece to a long side of the quilt. Trim angle to match pointed ends. Follow the Mitered Border directions on page 9 for attaching the short borders to the end points. Trim the wide angle even with the long edge.

FINISHING THE QUILT

✳ Quilt as desired and bind with the 2¼" wide strips.

DECEMBER:
Twelve Blocks, Twelve Peace on Earth

Finished size: 23" x 59" • Templates for this quilt are on pages 86-87.

Angels we have heard on high sweetly singing over the plains. Use checks and stripes for the angel wings and more border stripes for their dresses.

FABRIC SUPPLIES

❋ Light background	1⅛ yards
❋ Yellow stars	¼ yard
❋ Blue floral	½ yard
❋ Yellow pin dot	⅛ yard
❋ Assorted mediums/ darks	22 fat eighths
❋ Geometrics, stripes, checks, plaids	12 pieces 5" x 9"
❋ Blue floral binding	Included above
❋ Backing	1¾ yard
❋ Batting	

CUTTING INSTRUCTIONS

From light background fabric cut
- ✿ 1 piece, 5" x 34"
- ✿ 2 pieces, 5" x 35½"
- ✿ 2 pieces, 5" x 43"
- ✿ 32 squares, 2" x 2" for star corners
- ✿ 16 squares, 2¾" x 2¾" and cut twice on the diagonal for star points
- ✿ 2 strips, 2" x width of fabric for checkerboard

From yellow star fabric cut
- ✿ 1 strip, 5" x width of fabric
- Subcut into:
- ✿ 2 pieces, 5" x 6½"
- ✿ 2 pieces, 5" x 3½"
- ✿ 7 pieces, 5" x 2"

From assorted dark fabrics cut
- ✿ 16 squares, 2¾" x 2¾" and cut twice on the diagonal for star points
- ✿ 8 squares 2" x 2" for star centers
- ✿ From blue floral fabric cut
- ✿ 2 strips, 2" x width of fabric for checkerboard
- ✿ 4 strips, 2¼" x width of fabric for binding

MAKING THE STARS

* Sew the star point triangles into 32 quarter squares.

* Sew a quarter square to each side of a star center.

* Sew a star corner to each side of a quarter square and add to the top and bottom of the star centers.

MAKING THE 9 PATCH CHECKERBOARD

* Cut blue and light background strips in half across the fold.
* Sew the half strips in sets of 3 strips 2 different ways:
* Light-Dark-Light and Dark-Light-Dark.

* Make nine 9 patches.
* 9-patch A: dark outside corners. Make 3.
* 9-patch B: light outside corners. Make 6.

APPLIQUÉ OF THE ANGELS AND THE STARS

* Trace, fuse and appliqué angels and small stars.

ASSEMBLING THE QUILT

* Assemble the quilt in 5 vertical columns.

Column 1

* 6½" yellow star fabric, a star, 2" yellow star fabric, 3 angels, a B 9-patch.

Column 2

* 3½" yellow star fabric, a star, 2" yellow star fabric, a star, 2" yellow star fabric, 2 angels, a B 9 patch, an A 9 patch.

Column 3

* A star, 2" yellow star fabric, a star, 2 angels, a B 9 patch, an A 9 patch, a B 9 patch.

Column 4

* Same as column 2.

Column 5

* Same as column 1.

* Sew the 5 columns together to complete the quilt top.

FINISHING THE QUILT

* Quilt as desired and bind with the 2¼" wide strips.

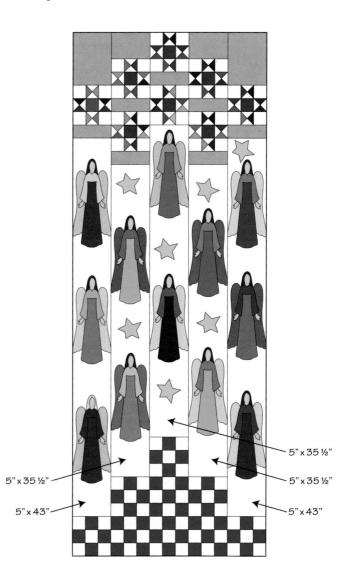

5" x 35 ½"

5" x 35 ½"

5" x 35 ½"

5" x 35 ½"

5" x 43"

5" x 43"

Thirteen Blocks, A Baker's Dozen

Finished size: 42" x 42" • Note: There are no templates for this quilt.

You have a baker's dozen in classic red and green with frosty white.

This quilt would be perfect on a table for a cookie exchange.

FABRIC SUPPLIES

* ❄ White on red dot   8" square
* ❄ Red on white dot   8" square
* ❄ Light background   1¼ yards
* ❄ Assorted Reds & Greens   To equal 1¼ yards
* ❄ Red binding   ⅜ yard
* ❄ Backing   1½ yard
* ❄ Batting   46" x 46"

2"

4"

6"

8"

10"

CUTTING INSTRUCTIONS

* ✿ A. From white on red dot fabric cut
* ✿ 9 squares, 2" x 2" for A centers
* ✿ B. From red on white dot fabric cut
* ✿ 4 squares, 2" x 2" for B centers
* ✿ 4 squares, 2⅜" x 2⅜" and cut once on the diagonal for half centers
* ✿ 1 square, 2¼" x 2¼" and cut twice on the diagonal for corner centers

From light background fabric cut

* ✿ 27 strips, 1½" x width of fabric

Leaving the fabric folded so you are cutting pairs, subcut into the following sizes and pile in 8 separate stacks for each size adding 2 pieces to each stack 9 times.

* ✿ 2"
* ✿ 4"
* ✿ 4"
* ✿ 6"
* ✿ 6"
* ✿ 8"
* ✿ 8"
* ✿ 10"

From assorted red and green fabric cut

✿ 27 strips, 1½" x width of fabric
✿ Leaving the fabric folded so you are cutting pairs, subcut into the following sizes and pile in 8 separate stacks for each size, adding 2 pieces to each stack 9 times.

Same fabric
✿ 2"
✿ 4"

Same fabric
✿ 4"
✿ 6"

Same fabric
✿ 6"
✿ 8"

Same
✿ 8"
✿ 10"

2"

4"

6"

8"

10"

From red binding fabric cut

✿ 5 strips, 2¼" x width of fabric

BLOCK ASSEMBLY

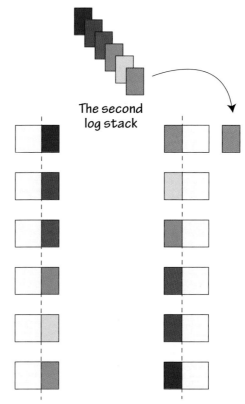

The second log stack

* Begin with stack of 9 Center A squares and the first stack of light background logs, 1½" x 2". Sew the first log to the square. Set the second log aside.
* Without cutting the thread on the sewing machine, sew the next log to another square and set the second log aside.
* Continue until you run out of squares.
* Now, turn the chain of squares and logs around. Sew the matching log to the other side of the square.
* The logs will all be in the correct order. Continue to the end.
* Clip both threads and press away from the center.

Center B Blocks   **Center A Blocks**

Round 1   Round 1

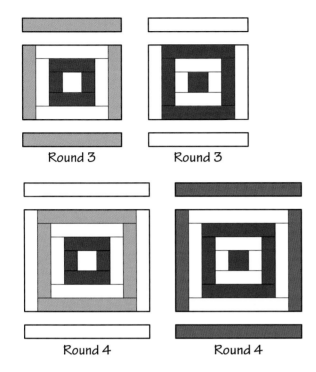

Round 3   Round 3

Round 4   Round 4

* Now, do the same with the first stack of 1½" x 4" logs.
* Match the log fabric to the first 2 logs.
* Sew one log on, set one aside.
* When you reach the end, turn around and sew on the second side.
* Clip the threads and press.
* This completes Round 1 for the Center A blocks.

* Repeat this method for the 4 Center B blocks.
* Round 1 for the Center B blocks will be assorted color logs.
* Using the diagram as a guide, continue until all the logs are sewn.

* Do the same with 8 B Triangle Centers and build 8 half blocks.

* Do the same with 4 B Triangle Centers and build 4 quarter blocks.

Make 8

Make 4

ASSEMBLY OF THE QUILT
* Sew the blocks in diagonal rows.
* Trim the excess from the half blocks.
* Sew on the 4 quarter block corners.

FINISHING THE QUILT
* Quilt as desired and bind with the 2¼" wide strips.

ASSEMBLY DIAGRAM

Templates

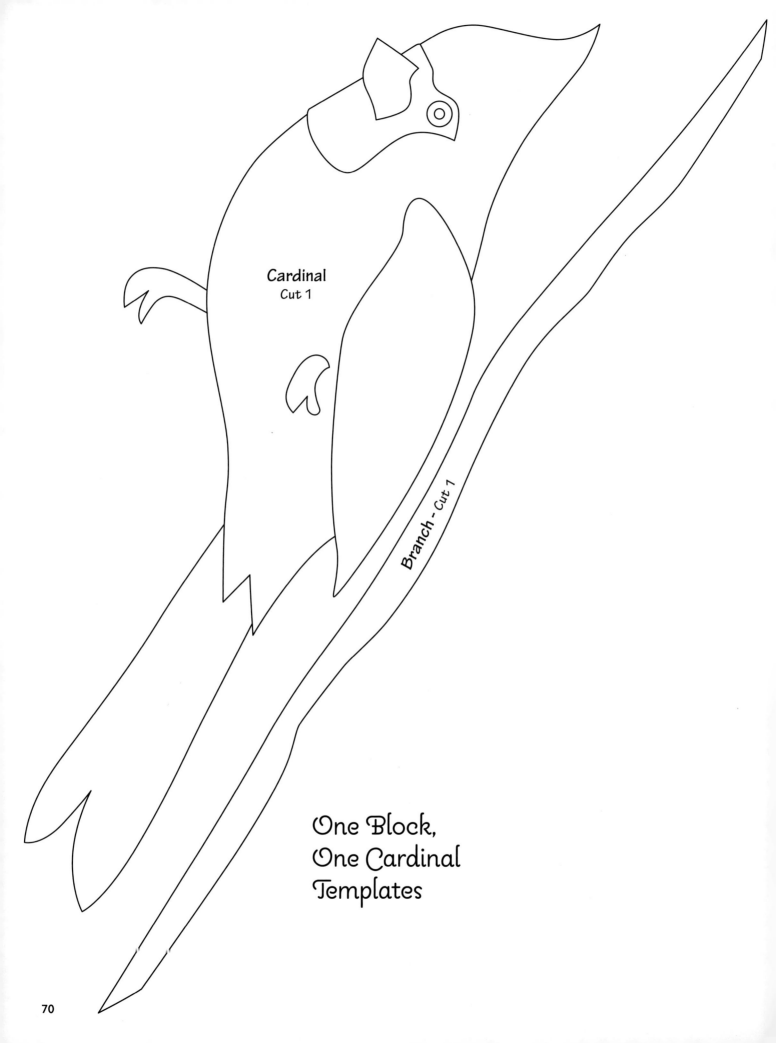

Cardinal
Cut 1

Branch – Cut 1

One Block,
One Cardinal
Templates

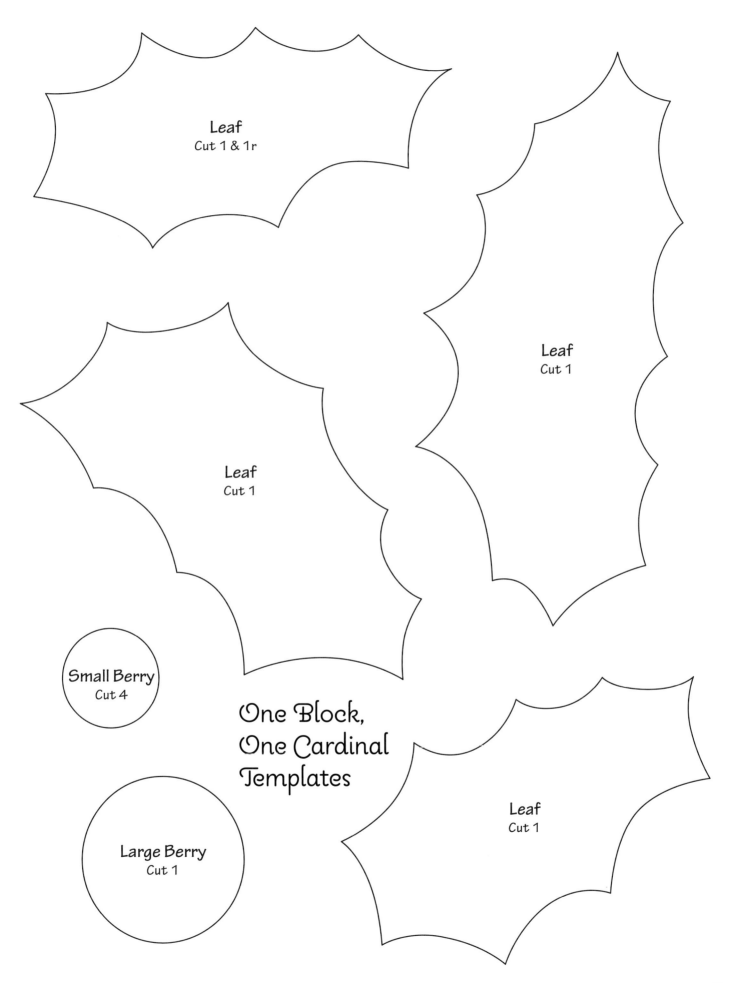

Leaf
Cut 1 & 1r

Leaf
Cut 1

Leaf
Cut 1

Small Berry
Cut 4

One Block,
One Cardinal
Templates

Large Berry
Cut 1

Leaf
Cut 1

Flower Pot
Cut 2

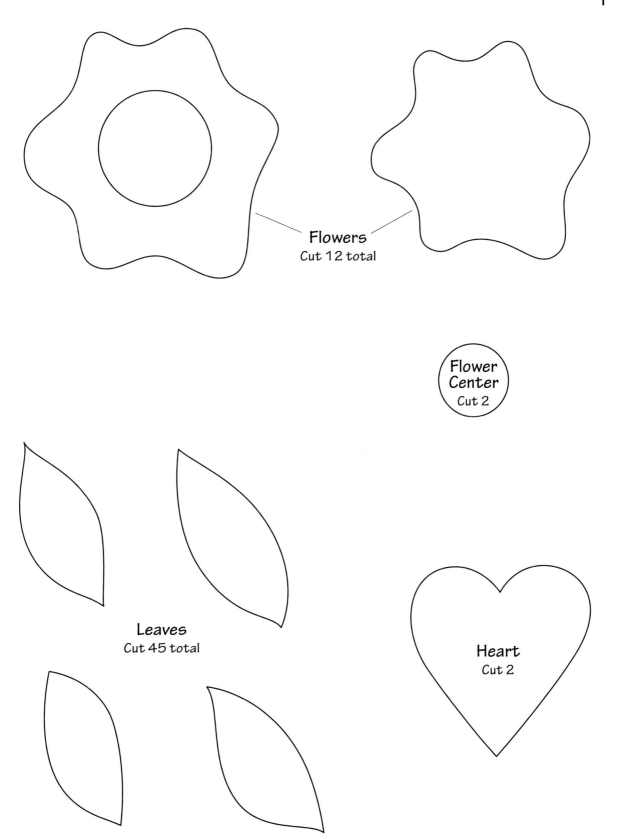

Flowers
Cut 12 total

Flower
Center
Cut 2

Leaves
Cut 45 total

Heart
Cut 2

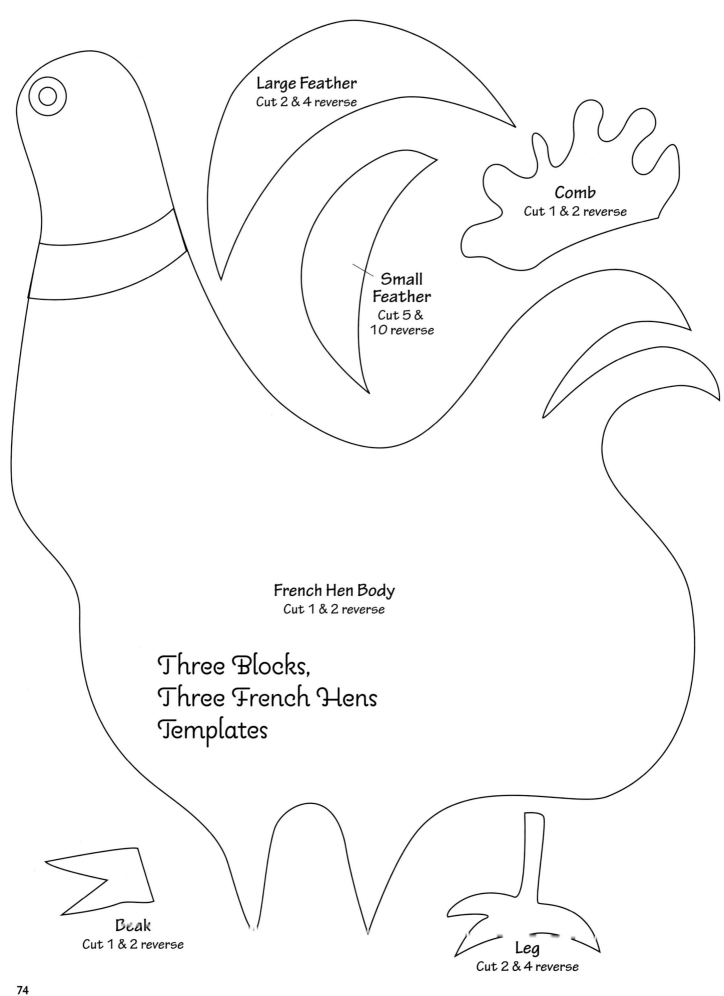

Large Feather
Cut 2 & 4 reverse

Comb
Cut 1 & 2 reverse

Small
Feather
Cut 5 &
10 reverse

French Hen Body
Cut 1 & 2 reverse

Three Blocks,
Three French Hens
Templates

Beak
Cut 1 & 2 reverse

Leg
Cut 2 & 4 reverse

Tulip
Cut 4

Leaf
Cut 216

Flower
Cut 4

Berry
Cut 4

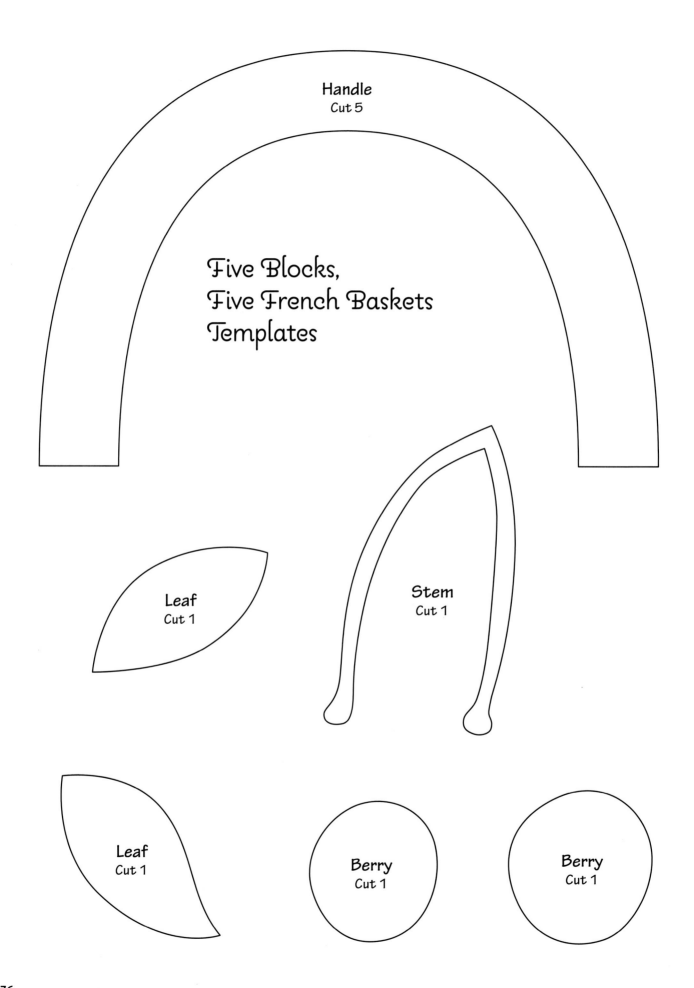

Handle
Cut 5

Five Blocks,
Five French Baskets
Templates

Leaf
Cut 1

Stem
Cut 1

Leaf
Cut 1

Berry
Cut 1

Berry
Cut 1

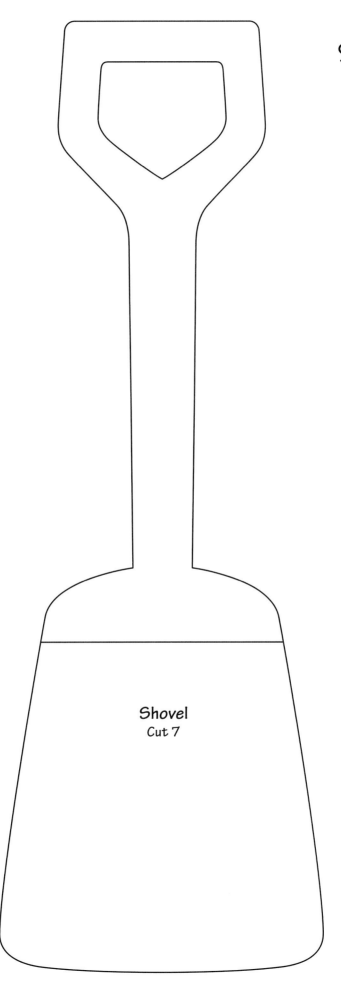

Shovel
Cut 7

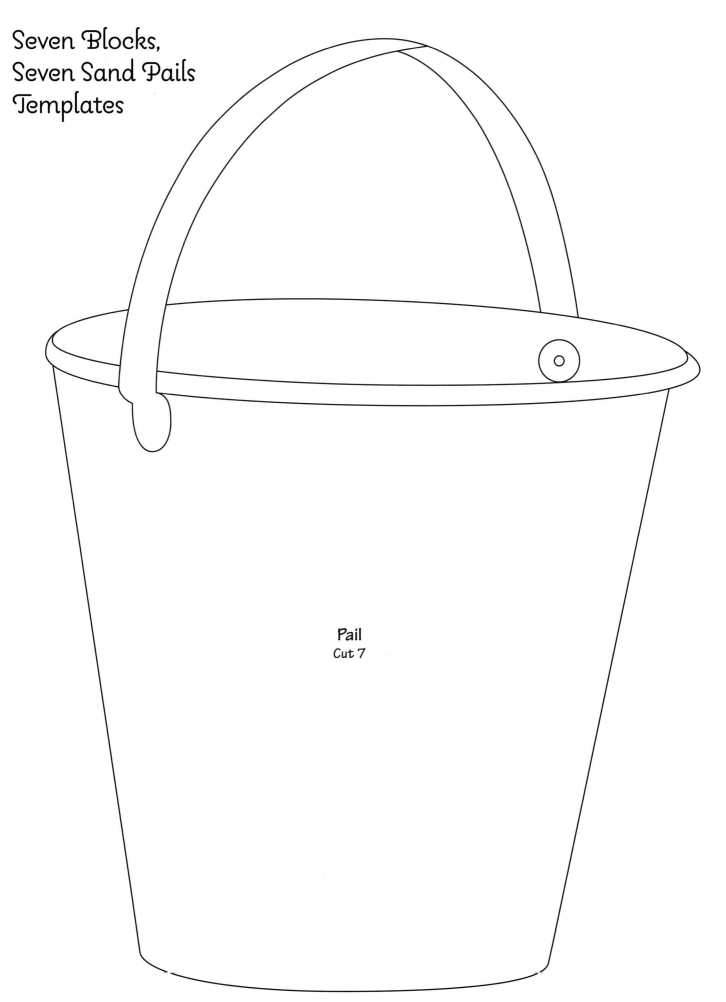

Pail
Cut 7

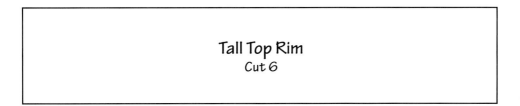

Tall Top Rim
Cut 6

Short Top Rim
Cut 3

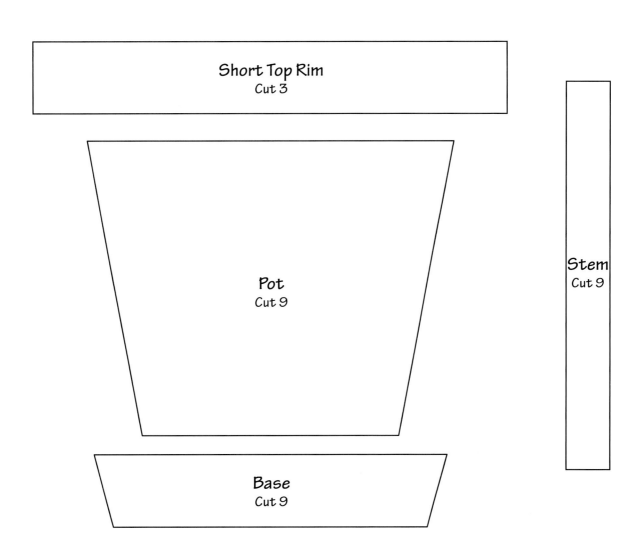

Stem
Cut 9

Pot
Cut 9

Base
Cut 9

Fleur de lys
Cut 1

Cherries
Cut 1

French Hen
Cut 3

Ten Blocks, Ten Favorite Things
Templates

Sunflower Leaf
Cut 1

Sunflower Leaf
Cut 1

Sunflower Leaf
Cut 1

Sunflower Leaf
Cut 1

Ten Blocks, Ten Favorite Things
Templates

Lime
Cut 1

Pear
Cut 1

Sunflower
Cut 1

Ten Blocks,
Ten Favorite Things
Templates

Olive Oil Jar
Cut 1

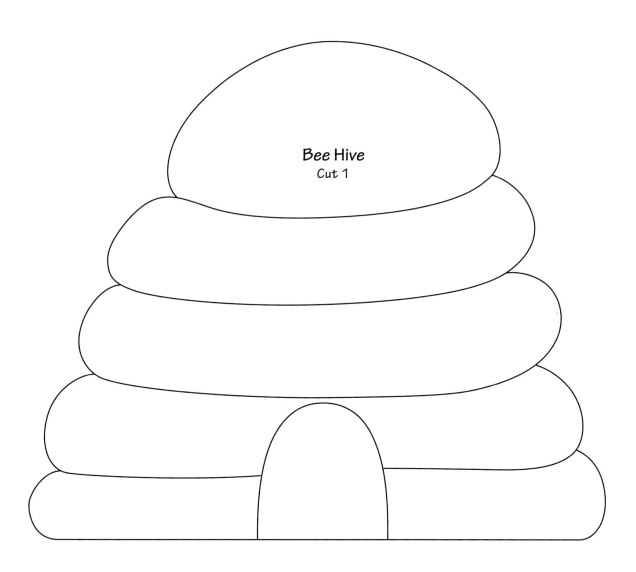

Bee Hive
Cut 1

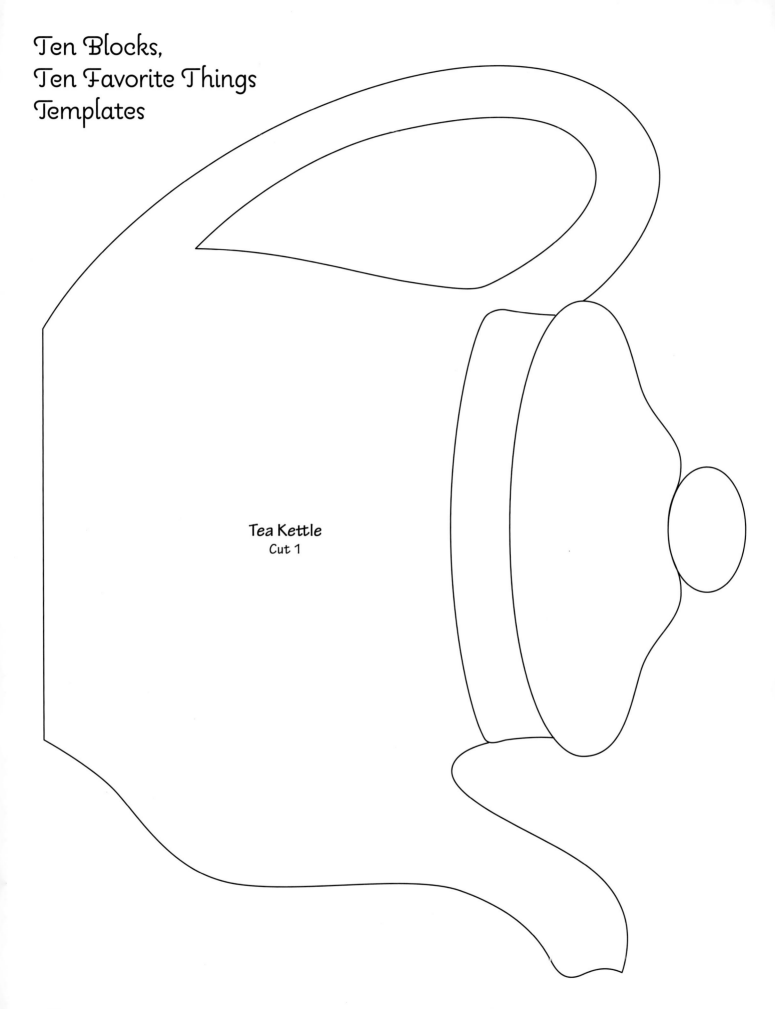

Tea Kettle
Cut 1

Round Leaf
Pineapple Top
Cut 4

Round Leaf
Pineapple Bottom
Cut 4

Pineapple
Cut 11

Ponted Leaf
Pineapple Top
Cut 7

Ponted Leaf
Pineapple Bottom
Cut 7

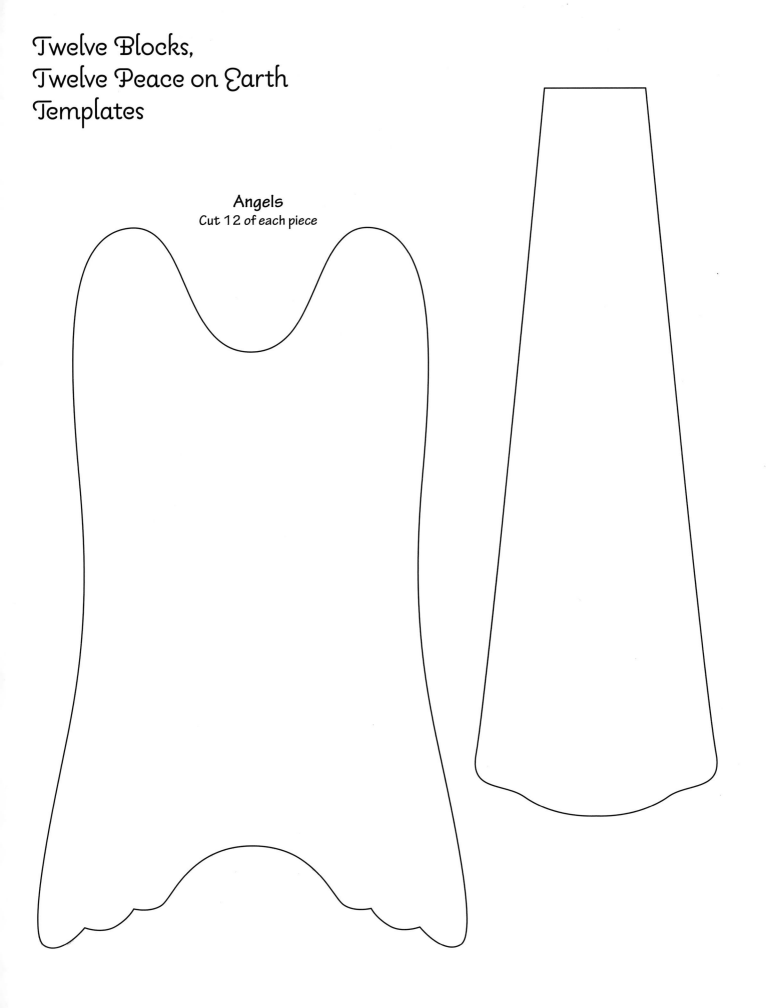

Angels
Cut 12 of each piece

Angels
Cut 12 of each piece

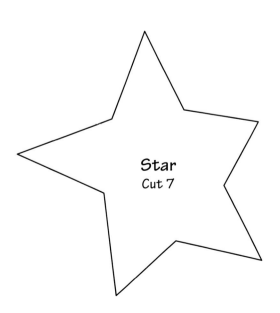

Star
Cut 7

RESOURCES
Sandy's fabrics are available at
Moda Fabrics
www.unitednotions.com

American Jane Patterns
64 Sandy Lane
Walnut Creek, CA 94597
www.americanjane.com
925-947-3977

OTHER KANSAS CITY STAR QUILTS BOOKS

Adventures with Leaders and Enders: Make More Quilts in Less Time! by Bonnie Hunter – 2010

A Bird in Hand: Folk Art Projects Inspired by Our Feathered Friends by Renee Plains – 2010

Feedsack Secrets: Fashion from Hard Times by Gloria Nixon – 2010

Greetings from Tucsadelphia: Travel-Inspired Projects from Lizzie B Cre8ive by Liz & Beth Hawkins – 2010

The Big Book of Bobbins: Fun, Quilty Cartoons by Julia Icenogle – 2010

Country Inn by Barb Adams and Alma Allen of Blackbird Designs – 2010

My Stars III: Patterns from The Kansas City Star, Volume III – 2010

Piecing the Past: Vintage Quilts Recreated by Kansas Troubles by Lynne Hagmeier – 2010

Stitched Together: Fresh Projects and Ideas for Group Quilting by Jill Finley – 2010

A Case for Adventures by Katie Kerr – 2010

A Little Porch Time: Quilts with a Touch of Southern Hospitality by Lynda Hall – 2010

Circles: Floral Applique in the Round by Bea Oglesby – 2010

Comfort Zone: More Primitive Projects for You and Your Home by Maggie Bonanomi – 2010

Leaving Baltimore: A Prairie Album Quilt by Christina DeArmond, Eula Lang and Kaye Spitzli from Of One Mind – 2010

Like Mother, Like Daughter: Two Generations of Quilts by Karen Witt and Erin Witt – 2010

Sew Into Sports: Quilts for the Fans in Your Life by Barbara Brackman – 2010

Under the Stars by Cherie Ralston – 2010

A Path to the Civil War: Aurelia's Journey Quilt by Sarah Maxwell and Dolores Smith of Homestead Hearth – 2010

Across the Wide Missouri: A Quilt Reflecting Life on the Frontier by Edie McGinnis and Jan Patek – 2010

Cottage Charm: Cozy Quilts and Cross Stitch Projects by Dawn Heese – 2010

My Stars IV: Patterns from The Kansas City Star, Volume IV – 2010

Roaring Through the '20s: Paper Pieced Quilts from the Flapper Era by Carolyn Cullinan McCormick – 2010